T0025373

How Do Spiders Walk on the Ceiling?

ANSWERING KIDS' QUESTIONS

by Nancy Dickmann

PEBBLE
a capstone imprint

Pebble Emerge is published by Pebble, an imprint of Capstone.
1710 Roe Crest Drive
North Mankato, Minnesota 56003
www.capstonepub.com

Library of Congress Cataloging-in-Publication Data
Names: Dickmann, Nancy, author.
Title: How do spiders walk on the ceiling? / Nancy Dickmann.
Description: North Mankato, Minnesota : Pebble, [2021] | Series: Questions and answers about animals | Includes bibliographical references and index. | Audience: Ages 6–8 | Audience: Grades 2–3 | Summary: "Spiders live everywhere! We even find them inside our homes. But how do they get way up on the ceiling? You have questions, and this book has the answers. Find out about spiders, including their body parts and behavior"—Provided by publisher.
Identifiers: LCCN 2020036386 (print) | LCCN 2020036387 (ebook) | ISBN 9781977131669 (hardcover) | ISBN 9781977132734 (paperback) | ISBN 9781977154361 (pdf) | ISBN 9781977156037 (kindle edition)
Subjects: LCSH: Spiders—Juvenile literature. | Spiders—Miscellanea—Juvenile literature. Classification: LCC QL458.4 .D483 2021 (print) | LCC QL458.4 (ebook) | DDC 595.4/4—dc23
LC record available at https://lccn.loc.gov/2020036386
LC ebook record available at https://lccn.loc.gov/2020036387

Image Credits
Getty Images: John Mitchell, 9; NASA: 19; Newscom: Boris Roessler/dpa/picture-alliance, 18; Science Source: Oliver Meckes/EYE OF SCIENCE, 10; Shutterstock: Amy Johansson, 17, Cathy Keifer, 7, 15, CyrilLutz, 14, Fadlan Hamid, 13, fukume, 6, lfdf, 20, moj0j0, 20–21 (spiders), Monkey Business Images, 5, ndarboy, design element, nico99, 8, owatta, design element, Spok83, 11, Vinicius R. Souza, Cover

Editorial Credits
Editor: Megan Peterson; Designer: Ted Williams; Media Researcher: Jo Miller; Production Specialist: Spencer Rosio

All internet sites appearing in back matter were available and accurate when this book was sent to press.

Printed and bound in the USA. 3837

Table of Contents

Words in **bold** are in the glossary.

Walking Upside Down

It's nearly bedtime. You're reading a book in bed. Then you look up. There's a spider on the wall! The spider crawls up the wall. Then it moves across the ceiling. It can walk upside down! If you tried to do that, you would crash to the floor. How does the spider do it?

Spiders Everywhere

Spiders can walk on more than just ceilings. They walk everywhere! More than 40,000 kinds of spiders live on Earth. Some of them hang out in our yards and homes.

Spiders live in many different places. Some spiders live in **deserts**. Some live near lakes and ponds. Others live in **rain forests**. They walk up tree trunks and along branches.

Don't Call Me Insect!

Spiders have eight legs for walking. This means they are not **insects**. Insects have only six legs. Spiders are **arachnids**. They are related to ticks and scorpions.

Spiders need to move around to catch **prey**. Most spiders eat insects. Larger spiders sometimes eat lizards or fish. Some even eat frogs, mice, or birds!

Fabulous Feet

Each spider foot is covered in hair. And each hair has lots of smaller hairs. The tips are shaped like triangles. These hairs are tiny. You need a **microscope** to see them.

hairs on the foot of a spider

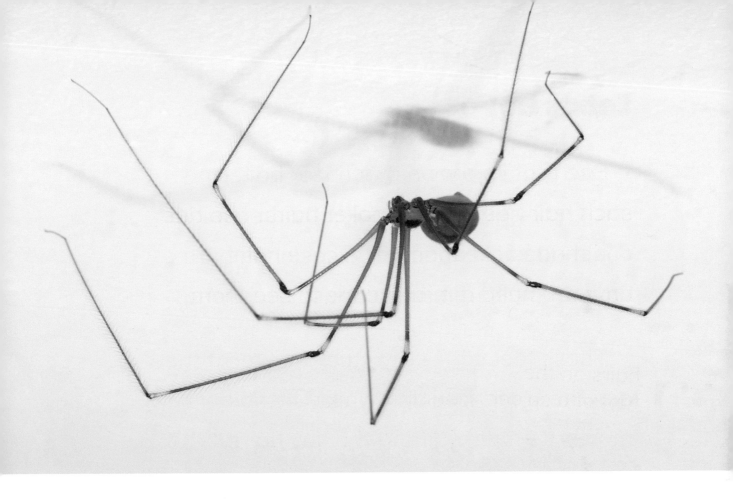

When a spider walks, something
special happens. First, its feet touch
down. Then the hairs stick to the surface.
The hairs act almost like tiny magnets!

Let It Go

See that spider on the fence? Its feet stick really tightly. In fact, 150 other spiders could ride on its back. The spider still wouldn't fall off! Its grip is just too strong.

Those feet can't stay stuck forever. If they did, the spider couldn't walk. The spider moves its foot by lifting the tiny hairs. But it has to lift the hairs one at a time. It can't lift them all at once.

Wonderful Webs

Is the spider in the middle of the ceiling? Or is it in a corner? Spiders love corners. It's dark there. They can easily see prey. Corners are also good places to build webs.

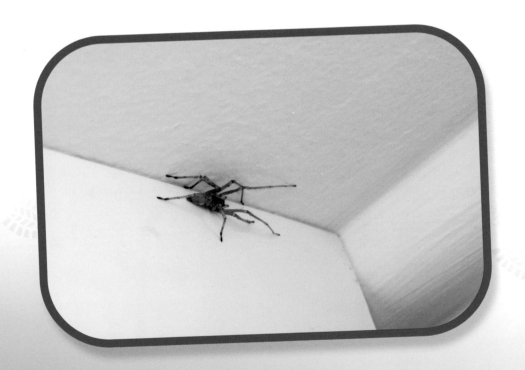

A spider's body makes **silk**. Many spiders spin it into webs. The silk is very strong. It is sticky too. Insects get stuck when they touch it. Then the spider chomps!

Don't Get Stuck!

Spiders walk across their own webs. They grab prey and fix rips. But they never get stuck! Spiders walk on the tips of their feet. They barely touch the silk.

Some parts of the web are made from a different kind of silk. It isn't sticky. The spider can rest there without getting stuck.

The Real Spider-Man?

Could people walk on the ceiling?
One day we might! Scientists study
spiders. They plan designs using tiny hairs.
We could have spider-hair sticky notes.
Or spider-hair gloves!

Astronauts could use tiny hairs too.

What if space suits were covered in hairs?

Astronauts could easily stick to things.

They wouldn't float away!

Go on a Spider Safari

What You Need:

- camera or sketchbook
- pencils or markers

What You Do:

1. Pick a spring or summer morning to go outside. Webs may be covered in dew. They will be easier to see. Ask an adult to come with you.

2. Look in sheds and garages. Search under outdoor furniture and in wood piles. Check gardens and plants.

3. When you find a spider, don't get too close! Some spiders have a nasty bite.

4. Take pictures or draw what you see. What is the spider doing? Does it have a web? How many spiders can you find?

Glossary

arachnid (uh-RACK-nid)—a group of animals that includes spiders, scorpions, mites, and ticks

astronaut (AS-truh-nawt)—a person who is trained to live and work in space

desert (DEH-zuhrt)—a dry area with little rain

insect (IN-sekt)—a small animal with a hard outer shell, six legs, three body sections, and two antennae; most insects have wings

microscope (MYE-kruh-skohpe)—a tool that makes very small things look large enough to be seen

prey (PRAY)—an animal hunted by another animal for food

rain forest (RAYN FOR-ist)—a thick forest where rain falls nearly every day

silk (SILK)—a thin but strong thread made by spiders

Read More

Murray, Laura K. *Spiders*. Mankato, MN: Creative Education/ Creative Paperbacks, 2016.

Pringle, Laurence. *Spiders!: Strange and Wonderful.* Honesdale, PA: Boyds Mills Press, 2017.

Spanier, Kristine. *Garden Spiders*. Minneapolis: Bullfrog Books, 2019.

Internet Sites

DK Find Out!: Spider
www.dkfindout.com/uk/animals-and-nature/arachnids/ spiders/

San Diego Zoo: Spiders
animals.sandiegozoo.org/animals/spider

Index